How Can This Be *Fair*?

DONALD A. WRIGHT

Cover Design:
Veronica Hawbaker, VeeDesign

Published by Serenity Publishing & Communications,
P.O. Box 282282, Nashville, Tennessee, 37228.

Unless otherwise noted Scripture quotations are taken from
THE NEW KING JAMES VERSION. Copyright 1979,
1980, 1982, Thomas Nelson, Inc., Publishers.

Scripture quotations noted in KJV are from the Holy
Bible, KING JAMES VERSION.

Library of Congress Catalog Number: 2003107626

ISBN 0-09712701-5-5

CONTENTS

CHAPTER ONE

"Dis-illusioned" With God

*1 It happened after this that the people
of Moab with the people of Ammon, and
others with them besides the Ammonites,
came to battle against Jehoshaphat.
2 Then some came and told
Jehoshaphat, saying, "A great multitude
is coming against you from beyond the
sea, from Syria; and they are in Hazazon
Tamar" (which is En Gedi).*
(2 Chronicles 20:1-2 NKJV)

It was an amazing and exciting season in
our lives in the tender years of our first pastorate. We were young enough to believe everything that we read in God's word. We had a
small congregation and as with any new work
we were met by challenges, but we were strong
in faith. After all, we had seen the supernatural
favor of God and experienced His presence
manifested in healed cancers and vanquished
tumors. We celebrated the greatness of God
with medical doctors as they confirmed His
miraculous intervention. All seemed to be in
order—we seemed to be in the center of God's

purpose and plan with nowhere to go but up. We were all excited and growing in faith in what God could do.

About six months into our ministry, we received a notice from a local attorney suggesting that there was a delinquency in our payment of the note covering our church facility, and that the lender was now demanding payment in full. Reading that letter was like some kind of bad dream—a terrible hoax being played on us. Surely this had to be a mistake. We checked our records thoroughly and presented the proof that we had paid the note on time. We discovered to our horror that the previous ministry from whom we had assumed the note had signed a contract with a small clause that allowed the financier to call in the loan in this manner.

We were in total disbelief and shock. Had we not truly experienced the power and presence of God in this place? We had everything in the proper order. We were experiencing great miracles, love, unity, peace, growth and blessings in every way in this work. We had been good stewards of God's money and had not wasted or mismanaged the resources He entrusted to us, and now this! God, how could you allow this to happen? *How could this be fair?*

I imagine that this was the same question formed on the lips of Jehoshaphat as he received the news of the imminent invasion of the Moabites, Ammonites, and Edomites.

Just as things were getting on the right track, the enemy crossed his frontiers. The *"after this"* in 2 Chronicles 20:1 refers to strong words and deeds by Jehoshaphat as he moved his nation toward revival in their relationship with Yahweh. Jehoshaphat had repented for any involvement with the enemies of God. He had cut down Ashtoreth and brought the people back to God out of their idolatry and *"set his heart to seek the Lord."* (2 Chronicles 19:3) What more could he or anyone else do than to tear down false gods and dedicate themselves to God? Jehoshaphat not only said the right things; he put feet to them by establishing truth and justice in the land. He was saying all the right things and making all the right moves and his heart was in all of them. How then could God respond by allowing this invasion? *How can this be fair?*

Perhaps the key to the invasion was not the ambitions of the pagan invaders, but in Jehoshaphat seeking after God. God gives us a guarantee as to our seeking after Him. He says that if we seek Him that He will let us find Him. (Jeremiah 29:13) The problem is that we seldom find the God we set out for. We find a God who is eminently bigger and more compli-

9

cated than we expected. He cannot be reduced to our puny understandings nor can He be influenced by our formulated requests. God is not a man! When we are confronted with the Living God, all of our understandings and all of our doctrines seem like some kind of an incomplete illusion of God. So we might say that when we seek God and find Him in all of His surpassing glory that we become "dis-illusioned" with God. And that is a good thing. I don't want an illusion of God; I want God!

Our confrontation with God is a personal rather than a corporate thing. Notice that the ones who brought the message of impending doom to Jehoshaphat stepped aside saying, *"a great multitude is coming against you."* There was no "us" mentioned here. Jehoshaphat was facing the enemy alone. Alone is how most of us feel when God seems to turn aside to allow problems in paradise. We ask, "God, don't you see what's happening here? Don't you care that the enemy is going to destroy me along with your own reputation?"

I asked God the same kinds of questions when our first church building was sold out from under us. As I stood on the courthouse steps watching our building being auctioned to the highest bidder I felt alone and helpless. I was sure that somehow God was going to intervene—that He was just expanding our faith somehow and that He would come through in some miraculous way like the cavalry riding over the hill in an old western movie. Maybe someone would just buy the building for us. Maybe God would somehow provide the funds for us to buy it. God would come through for us—somehow—some way. But the gavel fell in the calm silence of a business transaction without the benefit of bugles and victorious shouts. All hope seemed to vanish along with my understanding of God.

When we are "dis-illusioned" with God we feel alone, but also guilty somehow. We have been trained and conditioned to believe that if we pray the right way and with the right spirit that we can bend or influence God to move on our behalf. We have heard decades of teaching on having the right kind of faith. When life does not equal our prayer requests we feel as though the problem is in us. We have heard so many times that *"the effective fervent prayer of the righteous accomplishes much."* (James 5:16) So we deduce that because we experience difficulty or unheeded prayer that we must be unrighteous. How limited our understanding of God is.

God did not take our building because we had failed Him in some way any more than He did not send the enemy attack on Jehoshaphat because of some failure. The attack had nothing to do with performance; it had to do with Moabites, Ammonites and

Edomites. In both cases, God was out to destroy incomplete understanding and false notions of Him. God is out to "dis-illusion" us.

The Moabites and Ammonites were the product of the incestuous union of Lot and his daughters. (Genesis 19:37-38) Lot and his family were delivered from impending doom in Sodom, a place of great carnal sin and abomination. Lot's wife was turned into a pillar of salt as she looked back after fleeing the destruction, so Lot and his daughters were alone—cut off from the past and the future. The daughters of Lot who had no husbands, could not give Lot any grandchildren to carry on his lineage, so they decided to get their father drunk and sleep with him themselves. They took it upon themselves to continue Lot's name. The result was two nations born out of incest and sin who would forever live just outside of the promises of God.

The Moabites and Ammonites point to self-effort and self-confidence. They are filled with the pretense of good intention, but they attempt to wrestle power from God's hand and take it into their own. Moabites and Ammonites represent ideas that seem to make human sense at the time, but in the end have no true power or anointing. A million good ideas of how God could serve our purpose ran through my head as I stood on those courthouse steps, but in the end, God had His own plan, which would be carried out His way. If God would have heeded to my prayers, regardless of how well intentioned, I would have been the one in control, not God. Yes, God would get some glory, but so would my "anointed prayers." God needs to have *all* the glory. God will not share His glory with anyone else. He says, *"I am the LORD, that is My name; And My glory I will not give to another, nor My praise to graven images."* (Isaiah 42:8)

Along with the Moabites and Ammonites rode the Edomites, the ones from Mount Seir. They were descendants of Esau; the one who traded in his birthright and eternal blessings for a pot of soup. This people represents those who are not in proper standing with God and cannot advance past the thought that they missed there blessing and cannot understand why you should be allowed to enjoy yours in peace. They are the influence of the immediate that is opposed to the eternal. We in the American Church today are more into soul not spirit, position not power, magic and not ministry. When we get ourselves into a jam we want God to pull another rabbit out of His hat. We mutter scriptural incantations of prosperity and demand that God meet our objectives, as we understand them. The problem is that we really don't understand them. It is as though we are standing outside a great banquet hall and praying for another burger from our favorite fast food restaurant. We *need* a larger view of

13

God. We *need* a deeper trust in His heart. We
need to become "dis-illusioned" with God.

As I watched them auction our building,
I fought back both tears and anger. I was angry
with those who sold us the building under false
pretenses, I was angry with myself for getting
into the problem in the first place, and yes, also
angry with God. When the sale was over a
choice lay before me. I could choose to believe
that God was unfair or maybe that I had not
prayed in the right way, or I could choose to
trust in the heart of God and pursue Him
harder. This was the same God who had delivered me from my own struggles and sin. He
had lifted me out of drug abuse and danger and
protected me when guns were pointed at my
head or when I fell asleep at the wheel of my
car going 90 miles per hour. I had to believe
that this same God could also get me off those
courthouse steps and that His purpose would
continue regardless of my opinions and confu-
sion. Pruned from my own opinions of God's
purpose, our small congregation headed into
the home of one of the members where we
worshiped faithfully in a two-car garage for 18
months. We had to use noisy electric heaters in
the winter and leave the doors open in the
summer, but we grew strong in the presence of
the Lord in a way that we had never before
experienced. In His own time and for His own
glory, God provided a building for us when we
outgrew the garage. When we outgrew that

building the Lord blessed us with our very own edifice, which we built from the ground up. Here now was a new structure, with new walls, new carpet, new paint, and a new revelation of the ways of God. *God evicted us from our own illusion and brought us into His destiny!*

Along with a larger revelation of God came a less pleasant revelation of our own pride. We asked God how the loss of our building might affect His name, but in reality it was my own reputation that was on the block. God does not need us to defend His good name, but to depend upon it. All pride in ourselves must die if we are to gain a larger revelation of God. In the beginning of our own ministry we had faith in what God could do, and faith in the prayers that we prayed, but not faith in the heart of God.

Beloved, if you have picked up this book to gain an understanding of God's fairness you are on your way to being "dis-illusioned" with God. Whether you are experiencing some kind of trauma or great loss, or just cannot seem to find your way out of the miry clay of your circumstance, God is calling you—drawing you to Himself. When God is finished there will be nothing left but God and no Moabites or Ammonites, or Edomites in sight. We will say with Job, *"Though He slay me, yet will I trust Him."* (Job 13:15)

15

CHAPTER TWO

Coming to the End of Ourselves

*Then some came and told Jehoshaphat,
saying, "A great multitude is coming
against you from beyond the sea, from
Syria; and they are in Hazazon Tamar"
(which is En Gedi).* (2 Chronicles 20:
1-2)

During a recent counseling session I was
reminded of how my notion of the fairness of
God has changed. I was sitting with a minister
who was struggling with various aspects of his
ministry and life in general. The man who was
sitting opposite me was of the opinion that God
was somehow being unfair to him. As he told
me of his troubles he adopted a posture that
could be described as near arrogance, out of
which he told me in no uncertain terms that I
could not possibly understand his situation
because I "had it so good."

As I heard the man's words I wondered
to myself, "Who is he talking about?" I shared
with my fellow minister a game that we used to
play in my home with our children during
family times. We sat on the floor together
counting pennies and the first one to reach fifty

was the winner. Our children, like many children, gave no thought to the serious nature of the game; they just enjoyed sitting on the floor with their parents playing a game. What my children didn't know, however, was that they were counting pennies so their parents could run to the grocery store under cover of darkness to buy just a few little things.

The reality was that we had very little money and I felt guilty because I was preaching about the promise of prosperity for the faithful in God. I didn't dare let anyone see me in the store with rolls of pennies buying bread and milk. During those times my mouth was saying, "all is well," but my heart was muttering *"HOW CAN THIS BE FAIR?"* I remember well those nights, standing at the counter of the grocery store incognito thinking about how hard I was working and how little God was paying. I admit that there was a hint of bitterness in me as I sometimes felt overlooked by God. The problem was mine, not God's. I believed that God only loved me and I Him when He was blessing me financially. I could only love Him or trust Him if I had money in my pocket. The irony was that while I was accusing God of unfairness, I was the one being unfair to God in extending to Him a very conditional love.

During the session, the Lord warmly reminded me that I was no longer sitting on the

floor playing the counting game with my
children. He had blessed us in so many ways,
but the greatest was the understanding that
God's love for me is not conditioned by my
performance, and that my love and worship of
Him need not be restricted by His provision.
Material blessing is not the sign of God's love
and approval. He loves me even when, and
perhaps even more, when I struggle because
those struggles turn me toward Him in total
dependence. The Lord showed me that I had
come to the end of myself and my own efforts
and understanding and began to love and trust
God unconditionally. I have learned that the
confrontations we have with trials and unfore-
seen enemy attacks ultimately become a confrontation with God.

Getting Personal

Our confrontation with problems and
stress is a personal rather than a corporate
thing. Notice that the ones who brought the
message of invasion to Jehoshaphat stepped
aside saying, " *a great multitude is coming
against you.*" There were no *us* mentioned
here. Jehoshaphat was facing the enemy personally. Remember that the enemies that
Jehoshaphat was facing, the Moabites, Ammonites, and Edomites, were representatives of
self-effort and *self-confidence*. They are the
enemies that God is determined to destroy in

us, but we must face them on a personal and individual basis. Self fights the battle for *self*. I am not so concerned about the unfairness of God; it's that I feel God is somehow being unfair to *me*!! The real problem is that many times we are self-centered rather than God-centered.

We must come to the end of our theories ourselves and about God's fairness. Fairness is a human concept based on very limited under-standing of God and what He is up to in eter-nity. God speaks to us through the prophet Isaiah saying, *"For My thoughts are not your thoughts, Nor are your ways My ways,"* de-clares the LORD. *"For as the heavens are higher than the earth, So are My ways higher than your ways And My thoughts than your thoughts."* (Isaiah 55:8-9) We face what we think are new threats or hardships, but they are not new to God. God never gasps in shock at the problems that befall us. We can rest in the knowledge that God is in control.

Jehoshaphat was facing a new enemy that he was not used to fighting. We are used to setting ourselves in battle in array—trusting our own strength. But God, who is bent on destroying the enemy of self-centeredness, will inevitably bring new challenges our way that require new levels of trust and revelation. Usually, when we face a crisis or some new attack, we reach for whatever worked the last

time. We put on a video from the last conference we attended, or maybe we play a tape of
worship music to try and get to a place beyond
the struggle. Some times maybe we turn on
Christian TV hoping to hear a preacher give the
answer to what we are experiencing. We discover in the end that we have heard all the
words and hummed all the tunes, but we still
feel alone abandoned as we face the enemy.

There is something missing in all the
familiar sources of comfort and the solutions
that worked the last time around. We find
nothing to energize our spirit—nothing to carry
us to a higher and more spiritual plane—nothing that brings us closer to God Himself. We
are still hungry and thirsty for more of God.
I'm not saying that the men and women of God
on those tapes and singing those songs aren't
anointed. I'm simply saying that this is a new
fight and a new enemy and nothing short of a
new and personal encounter with God is going
to fill my need.

Jehoshaphat came to the same point that
you and I come to where the issues of life have
challenged our knowledge of God. What he
was experiencing did not seem to agree with
what he believed about his relationship with
God. This new crisis has thrown him into a
battle for which he is untrained. He and the
nation stood naked and exposed before God
having no fig leaves to cover their vulnerabili-

ties. They came to a place that required a decision to turn either to themselves or toward God.

When we are confronting a new problem most of us cannot take our eyes off of ourselves and begin to look for something we did wrong or believed wrong or prayed wrong. We find ourselves somehow feeling guilty and ashamed which only serves to drive us farther away from God. I think here is a good place to remind ourselves bad things show up in the lives of good people. It has been suggested to the body of Christ by some gifted teachers, our faith is too weak or that we have a bad confession. But when my children are cutting up and getting into trouble I don't need someone to tell me that it's because I forgot to claim something or another. When the strong wind of a storm blows a tree through my roof it's not because of a failure in belief or incomplete coverage in prayer. In the midst of trial and tragedy I don't need anyone who has hyper-faith telling me I didn't claim something. It's not a failure, its life, and life comes with surprises both pleasant and unpleasant.

If I can get past my false guilt I may encounter self-effort. I sometimes feel that there are things in my life that I could fix myself if God would allow my timing and effort to suffice and leave them up to me. I start thinking and working my way out of problems and coming up with good ideas. I wonder what might have happened if Jehoshaphat, instead of praying, would have gotten the army together and said, *"Men I know we can win this thing. Yes the enemy is much stronger and we are surrounded on every side, but I am open for suggestions. How should we respond to this overwhelming attack?"* No, I don't think there would have been much power in any of that.

The best and only thing we can do when we experience a new attack is to trust God to handle the enemy. We call this radical trust humility. Humility is having a proper concept of God and ourselves. That may lead some to say that we are wimpy and not using the authority God has given to us. The opposite is true. God gives us armor and authority to stand in the face of the enemy. (Ephesians 6:13-14) It takes more guts to stand and wait for God than it does to just look busy and get slaughtered by the enemy. We must learn to stand before God in meekness and humility. We are not copping out of the fight; we are fighting alongside God!

Please don't mistake my meekness for weakness. Our puny and powerless self-efforts keep us focused on ourselves and not God. Distracted by our own efforts, we cease pursuing God and become slack in reading His word. We feel sorry for ourselves or ashamed and don't seek out counsel from other brothers and sisters in the body for fear they might discover that we have the same problems they have. We become sensual and forget the spiritual. To be meek is to be truly confident in God. It is the meek that inherit the earth, not the tired and defeated who war in their own power and intellect.

New Threats Bring New Direction

It is the direction in which we point our lives that determines the outcome of our confrontation with the enemy. We can either point ourselves to the flesh or the Spirit—toward ourselves or toward God. One direction leads to death and the other to life and peace even in the midst of great trial. Listen to the words of the Apostle Paul.

> *1 If then you were raised with Christ,*
> *seek those things which are above,*
> *where Christ is, sitting at the right hand*
> *of God. 2 Set your mind on things*
> *above, not on things on the earth...*
> Colossians 3:1-2

> *5 For those who live according to the*
> *flesh set their minds on the things of the*
> *flesh, but those who live according to the*
> *Spirit, the things of the Spirit. 6 For to*
> *be carnally minded is death, but to be*

*spiritually minded is life and peace.
7 Because the carnal mind is enmity
against God; for it is not subject to the
law of God, nor indeed can be.*
Romans 8:5-7

The main issue of our peace is what we
are seeking. If we are seeking things on the
earth, the carnal, then we can expect to be
derailed and attacked by the enemies whose
realm and authority are in the earthly realm.
We are the ones who choose the battleground;
it's up to us. If we are enamored with wealth
and worldly status we place ourselves in the
arena of the enemy. Yes, we are saved and in
the Kingdom, but this earth still lies under the
sway of the devil. 2 Corinthians 4:4 calls this
the domain of the *"prince of the power of the
air."* It seems that many times the very things
we are so focused on are the things that come
under attack. If we are focused on money we
will experience trouble in the realm of
finances. If we are worried about our kids
going out and getting into trouble it seems that
our kids invariably go out and get into trouble.

How then is this struggle decided? It is
decided when we take it out of the enemy's
hands. Notice that Jesus always picked His
own battles and did not wage war on ground
that He would lose. He stayed away from
places where they doubted Him, and He never

placed value on earthly wealth. In fact He said, *"Foxes have holes and birds of the air have nests, but the Son of Man has nowhere to lay His head."* (Matthew 8:20) The strategy is simple but we usually miss it. If we put value on something and consider it important then the enemy is going to go after that thing. But if we do as Paul says and set our minds, or focus on the things of God, the enemy cannot touch us. Its not to say that the things you care about are insignificant, however, the question must be asked are they yours or God's? Is He orchestrating it, or are you in charge and running the show.

What does this have to do with our concept of fairness? Everything! Those arenas where we feel unfairly attacked are superfluous to God—they are in His hand. If we say, "God you are being unfair in that I have no money." God replies, *I have all the money, why do you need your own*? If I say, "God I trusted you for this building and you allowed man to take it away." God replies, *"I give eternal life to you, and you will never perish; and no one will snatch you out of My hand."* (John 10:28) We choose the battleground, not the enemy, even though it may seem otherwise, our lives are *"hidden with Christ in God."* (Colossians 3:3)

The confrontation with the enemy is always a personal one and we cannot go through it by proxy. When Moab, Ammon, and Esau, the martial forces of self-centeredness appear on the horizon, and we are tempted to accuse God of unfairness, we must not war over ground that we are supposed to have already given up. As the enemy approached Jerusalem, Jehoshaphat remembered to whom the city and its people belonged. We must do the same. We must come to the end of our own opinions and ability and allow the Lord to defend what is His.

CHAPTER THREE

Afraid to Let Go

3 And Jehoshaphat feared, and set himself to seek the LORD, and pro-claimed a fast throughout all Judah. 4 So Judah gathered together to ask help from the LORD; and from all the cities of Judah they came to seek the LORD.
(2 Chronicles 20:3-4)

"*...Jehoshaphat feared.*" That's not what we wanted to hear. This great and righteous reformer king was afraid of the enemy. He should have had no cause to be afraid in that he obeyed God tearing down what should have been torn down and building up what should have been built up. But he did indeed *fear* the onslaught of the enemy.

Fear results when we are confronted with the unknown or the overwhelming—something beyond our control or understanding. Fear, like a roaring lion, rivets our attention to the source of the threat and does not allow us to turn away from it. Jehoshaphat was in *fear* because he was confronted with something beyond his ability to understand—beyond his experience. He was, at first, overwhelmed because he was focused on the enemy rather than God. But there was a decided shift from fear to victory by the end of the story. The shift away from fear was the result of a change in focus from the enemy to the Lord Himself; the only object worthy of fear. That shift takes place in us as we decide to let go of our own ability and understanding and hand ourselves over to the Lord in a radical trust.

Letting Go

When we teach a small child to swim they tend to want to hold onto the side of the swimming pool. The side of the pool represents safety to them—something they can hang onto. The problem is that if they hold onto the side of the pool they never learn to swim. We have to invite them to "let go" and trust themselves to our arms in water that is over their heads. They are in effect handing themselves over to us. Indeed there are many that never let go of the side of the pool who live their whole lives in fear.

When Jehoshaphat *"feared"* he decided to *let go* of the side of the pool. The scripture says that he *"set himself,"* which means that he handed himself over to God in trust. Jehoshaphat presented himself along with his fear and uncertainty to God. When the news of the impending invasion first arrived at his doorstep, fear might have taken control and thrown Jehoshaphat into the hand of the enemy. The enemy lives at the side of the pool reminding us how deep the water is and how we can't swim. But the Lord knows that we are in over our heads—that our toes cannot feel the bottom of the pool, and calls us to Himself. The next move however is up to us. We have to *let go*.

It's hard to *let go*. Many have said to me, "I don't want to lose all I have Pastor." When challenges come along we may have to *let go* of our position in the body of Christ, or we may have to *let go* of our understanding of God or our theology. We may have to *let go* of old offenses and past wounding in order to move to a new place of understanding in God. New obstacles deliver new opportunities and revelation. We must *let go* of anything that might keep us from growing in the Lord including our sense of what is fair and what is not fair—what makes sense and what does not.

One of the difficulties we have in approaching God when events seem to turn against the righteous is that we pray with one hand tied behind our backs. We never really *let go* and hand our lives over to God. We pray but then we add worry to our prayer at how God is going to work things out. It is like trying to swim while continuing to hang on to he side of the pool. James says that when we pray we must *"ask in faith, with no doubting, for he who doubts is like a wave of the sea driven and tossed by the wind. For let not that man suppose that he will receive anything from the Lord; he is a double-minded man, unstable in all his ways.* (James 1:6-8) James calls us *"double-minded,"* which is to say that we are trying to live by two different standards; God's and ours.

The reality is that we can only be set in one direction at a time. We will either be set toward God or us.

Setting Ourselves

The text says that Jehoshaphat "set himself", that is to say that he made a decision to point himself in a particular direction. It is the direction we point our lives that determines the outcome of our confrontation with the enemy. We can either point ourselves to the flesh or the Spirit—toward ourselves or toward God. One direction leads to death and the other to life and peace even in the midst of great trials.

Jehoshaphat made a monumental decision when his current experience and the threat of the enemy did not agree with his understanding of God. He opted to seek more of God. The scripture says that he set himself, or handed himself over, with the purpose of "*seek-ing the Lord.*" Jehoshaphat saw that there had to be more to this than what met the eye, so he looked for something beyond his own carnal perception and understanding into the very heart of God.

In his seeking more of God, Jehoshaphat proclaimed a fast. Literally, he closed his mouth with nothing going in and nothing com-ing out. There had to be something that he did not yet understand about God if the enemy was getting ready to crash through the door. Rather than accuse God of unfairness Jehoshaphat shut everything and everyone down to go after more of God. Not only did he fast, but also everything and everybody else in Judah fasted. If the head was seeking God so then must the rest of the body.

Fasting is not a way to make God feel sorry for us and fill our shopping lists. Fasting is *not* a holy hunger strike whereby we bend God's will to our will. Fasting is where we bend our heart to His heart. Fasting is *not* merely the abstaining from food or other worldly pleasure, it is a way to empty ourselves of any desire that challenges our desire to hear and commune with God.

When we, as strong and faithful believ-ers, encounter dire circumstances and we are tempted to accuse God of unfairness, we must learn to let go and to set ourselves to seek the Lord. Many times God is calling us to let go of the side of the pool just as when Jesus invited Peter to get out of the boat and come to Him on the water. (Matthew 14:27-32) No one has ever moved on to greater dimensions in God and stayed where they were. The "unfairness" that confronts us is an opportunity to grow closer to God if we will but let go and set ourselves to seek the Lord.

> *4 I sought the LORD, and He heard me, And delivered me from all my fears. 5 They looked to Him and were radiant, And their faces were not ashamed. 6 This poor man cried out, and the LORD heard him, And saved him out of all his troubles. 7 The angel of the LORD encamps all around those who fear Him, And delivers them. 8 Oh, taste and see that the LORD is good; Blessed is the man who trusts in Him! (Psalm 34:4-8)*

(*Who lets go and hands himself over to God.*)

CHAPTER FOUR

Making Room for God

*Then Jehoshaphat stood in the assembly
of Judah and Jerusalem, in the house of
the LORD, before the new court.*
(2 Chronicles 20:5)

Several years ago while I was pastoring a church in North Carolina, the Lord began to impress upon me that He was going to move us onto a new season of ministry. After much prayer, I discerned that I had heard the Lord clearly and proceeded to put the house on the market to move on to the Lord's next assignment. I felt led back to the Washington D.C. area, which was the area where I grew up. Though the prospect of returning to my hometown was intriguing, I had become accustomed to the comparatively lower cost of living in the South. Needless to say, the cost of replacing the housing space we were used to was going to be a challenge in the nation's capitol.

In what seemed to be a short period of time, we had a buyer for our beautiful home on the lake in North Carolina. The problem was now we had no place to go. I wrestled with the fear that we would sell our home and then have no place to live. We had yet to find a house that would meet our needs with in our price range. As we continued to pray about finding a new home the Lord instructed me to take the contract on our home and trust Him to make a way for our family. Of course I reminded the Lord time and again that this move was His idea in the first place. He assured me that we would be fine.

With the closing date on our North Carolina home fast approaching we decided to rent a small house until we could find what we were looking for. Unfortunately, the smaller house could not hold all of our things so we put them in storage while we continued to search for a permanent home. As life would have it, one of the worse floods in the history of the North Carolina area was about to take place. When the rains came, we were safely in church in Washington with our family safe from the flood, but the storage facility we rented to store 90 percent of our belongings was submerged beneath the floodwaters for a week. As the floodwaters subsided, our worst fears were confirmed; we lost everything we had in storage.

Here we were, commuting between North Carolina and Washington D.C. following the calling and direction of God, and we were wiped out. How is it that I had to sell our dream house on the lake and uproot our family to go to a new and uncertain future? We gave up or lost everything to obey God. I thought, *"How can this be fair?"*

No sooner were these words out of my mouth, I met Stan; a young realtor who had heard about our plight and was certain he could find suitable housing. We searched for many hours until we found what we wanted, but it was out of our price range. However, after days of negotiating, the sellers agreed to sell us the home at a price we could afford and saved us enough money to replace all that we lost in the flood.

Up until that time and those circumstances I felt pretty much in control of my life and ministry. I had given the Lord a measure of control over my life and ministry. What I was discovering however, was that it was His life and His ministry. When God called me to a new place in ministry, He also called me to a new place in Him. It was a place where I would have to trust Him to keep us where His Spirit had led us. I have since found the times when I believe life seems unfair it may be that I am moving into a new place in God. This new place is going to be a place of expanded trust and obedience in God. It is the place where I am least in control of what comes next and where God will get the glory for everything that happens. In reality, this new place is actually one that I built for God in my life through successive steps of surrender. God is moving in where I have made room for Him.

When Jehoshaphat was faced with what may have seemed like an unfair attack from the enemy, he set his attention and spirit to seek the Lord and then he moved to the "new court" in the temple. This was the most prominent and public place of the temple. This was the place between the outer court and the court of the priests. [1] He was standing in the place where the Levites played music for the temple services. This was the same court where Solomon stood and knelt to dedicate the temple to God and where they would call upon the Lord. It is a place between God and the world—the inner court and the outer court. This is the place where you and I stand as we turn toward God rather than away from Him in the face of what seems to be unfair in our lives.

A New Place in God

There are many ways we could describe this new place we have come to in God. The place where Jehoshaphat stood was a "new" or a remodeled place. He remodeled the court as part of his reform and religious renovations in Judah. He was in a sense making more room for God in the temple. Jehoshaphat looked around and saw that his new revelation of God was going to require a larger space for worship, which is the expression of what we know of God. It stands to reason that our worship must grow in accordance with our revelation. It should have been no surprise then that God would move in to the place that was expanded for His habitation.

This is not something strange; it is the place we have built for God. God is going to move into this new place we have built for Him and going to extend our revelation to an even greater level as He responds to the circumstances we find ourselves in. What Jehoshaphat knew about God when he received news of the attack and what he knew after the enemy was destroyed were very different. Jehoshaphat would learn the depths of God's faithfulness and power in ways that he could never learn in any other way.

We should not be surprised when we extend our faith to God that we may see things we have never seen before. In my own life, I had not yet experienced the reality of God's provision until I signed the contract and packed our bags to move out of one house not knowingwhere we were going. God would have no way to demonstrate that kind of faithfulness and provision if I just stayed where I was. My moving out of that comfortable dream house was a way to build a new place for God. I had to get out of the way to "make room" for God to reveal something new of Himself to me. God was not being unfair to me; He had already prepared something greater for our family than I could have imagined.

The new place that Jehoshaphat found himself in brought a new prayer and a new focus. All that he knew, or thought he knew of God, was becoming obsolete in the face of new challenges and new answers from God. When circumstances don't seem to add up, instead of accusing God, we need to make room for Him to move in a way that only He can and watch as He reveals new and previously unknown levels of love and faithfulness.

A Public Place

This new place in God where Jehoshaphat stood was also a very public place. Jehoshaphat stood in the same place where his ancestor Solomon stood to dedicate that very temple. The outer court was where the people,not the priesthood gathered. This was, for Jehoshaphat, a public display of humility before God. In approaching God this way all that Jehoshaphat knew and believed about God would be evident to the people of Judah.

What we do in the midst of crisis is a public demonstration of what we really believe about God. Consider when Peter and the others were thrown in jail by a bunch of jealous religious people.

17 Then the high priest rose up, and all those who were with him (which is the sect of the Sadducees), and they were filled with indignation, 18 and laid their hands on the apostles and put them in the common prison. 19 But at night an angel of the Lord opened the prison doors and brought them out, and said, 20 Go, stand in the temple and speak to the people all the words of this life."
(Acts 5:17-20)

Here were the very men who stood with Jesus those three plus years in ministry. They saw his wonders and heard his teaching. They saw him walk on water and saw him nailed to a cross. They saw Him raised, glorified and ascending into Heaven. Peter preached the most powerful and effective sermon in thehistory of the church on Pentecost and walked in the anointing of God to the extent that his mere shadow would heal the sick and tormented. But now, here is Peter thrown in jail.*How can this be fair?* Peter and the rest were coming to a new place in God.

41

What Peter did or did not do next was a public display of what he really knew and believed about God. We hear no talk of self-examination or self-pity or accusing God of unfairness. Peter and the others had made room for God to move in some other way as they were taken off to jail, and God sent His angels to open prison doors before them. Even though they had been witness to amazing events in the ministry of Jesus, there were new and even more powerful realms into which God would lead them. There are always new depths in God to be revealed. *"Oh, the depth of the riches both of the wisdom and knowledge of God! How unsearchable are His judgments and His ways past finding out!'* (Romans 11:33)

The next thing we know Peter and the others were back at the temple at the direction of God's messenger giving the people the words of life in Christ. They were qualified to give instruction because they were walking in that life—that new place they had made for God in their own lives. Everyone within ear-shot was drawn into that new place along with Peter.

As we make room for God to move and reveal his heart to us He crashes through prison doors where we have kept our previous revelation, crashing through old paradigms and blowing the doors off our understanding. As we respond to God's revelation of Himself the world will be drawn into greater depths of God with us. The new places we are building for God is a place of public display where all that we truly believe of God will be manifested and ultimately have its effect on the world through us.

A Place of Worship

Immediately behind the court where Jehoshaphat stood was the place where the Levites played music to accompany the temple service. This new place in God that Jehoshaphat built was the place of worship in its truest sense. Our worship of God is most real and genuine when it flows out of a heart totally desperate for God. This is the place where our worship of God becomes real and genuine. This new place in God is the place where our worship brings Earth to Heaven and Heaven to Earth.

Worship is reflecting the "worth-ship" of God back to Him. As we stand here on Earth in the midst of dire circumstances, lets seize the opportunity and focus on God rather than our challenges. Worship is not an attempt to manipulate God somehow, but rather to fill the place where we are with His presence rather than with our circumstances; where we bring

Heaven to Earth. Worship is the ultimate way of making room for God right here and right now.

This new place in God brings about new levels of worship of God because it reveals new levels of His love and awesome power. It is a place beyond the form of Godliness, where we walk in dependence upon God's power. (2 Timothy 3:5) It is the place where God is most real and our worship the most genuine.

A Place of Rest

The new place that Jehoshaphat and the people of Judah found themselves in was the ultimate place of rest in God. Until we come to the end of our own ability and discernment we live in constant striving and worry. Imagine what might have happened if the threat of the enemy had never materialized. Jehoshaphat and the people of Judah would have lived their lives in a lesser knowledge of God. They would have served a God who was a little smaller and a little less powerful. In the case of my own family, we may have stayed in thatdream house by the lake for years, content to pastor that precious group of people in North Carolina, but because we made room for God, we have been put in a position to minister to thousands of people in the heart of our nation's capitol. God brought us to a new place of ultimate rest in Him. Not to mention that destiny had already selected another great man to sit in the chair where I sat and do an even greater work. He called us to step out into the darkness of uncertainty and into a new light of His love and faithfulness. God is bringing us relentlessly to a place of rest in Him. It is the place that we ourselves have made for God. When we make room for His, He will fill it with Himself.

When we are tempted to believe that God is being unfair somehow, we must listen for the sounds of construction, because a new place is being made ready. It will be a place filled with the glory of God; the place of ultimate rest in God.

CHAPTER FIVE

The Promise of God

*6 ...and said: "O LORD God of our
fathers, are You not God in heaven, and
do You not rule over all the kingdoms of
the nations, and in Your hand is there
not power and might, so that no one is
able to withstand You? 7 Are You not our
God, who drove out the inhabitants of
this land before Your people Israel, and
gave it to the descendants of Abraham
Your friend forever? 8 And they dwell in
it, and have built You a sanctuary in it
for Your name, saying, 9 If disaster
comes upon us—sword, judgment,
pestilence, or famine—we will stand
before this temple and in Your presence
(for Your name is in this temple), and cry
out to You in our affliction, and You will
hear and save.'* (2 Chronicles 20:6-9)

When we find ourselves in a tight spot
we tend to go to God to remind Him of all that
He has promised us concerning our wellbeing
and personal prosperity. We memorize scrip-
tures that seem to unlock the vaults of Heaven
to meet our perceived needs. But as we focus
on the promises of God, we often miss the

47

promise of God's person—who God is. The promise of God is all that God is and will be to us in the tight places.

A promise is the expectation of receiving something in the future based on our experience in the past. We see the clear sky in the morning and we say that the day promises to be beautiful. The weather is an indication of what is to come based upon our past experiences. This is true of God as well. When the enemy attacks we remind ourselves of the promise of God. Jehoshaphat reminded himself of all that God is. He is the God of our fathers—the God of Heaven—the God over all nations—the God of all power and might—our God—the God who is present. All of these reflect the character of God that becomes collateral to our hope in our seasons of challenge.

When the enemy fell on Jehoshaphat and all of Judah, he began to remind himself and all the people Who God was. He was not seeking the fulfillment of God's promises as much as He was declaring something about the God he knew. He was not seeking God as Santa Claus; he was aligning himself with the very person and character of God.

As Solomon was praying his dedication of the Temple, He asked God no less than eight times to "hear from Heaven." (2 Chronicles 6) While there were several petitions in

Solomon's prayer, the underlying thought was that God would hear the cries of His people in distress and answer them according to His own loving-kindness. (2 Chronicles 6:42) Solomon relied upon the promise of God's person to meet the needs of the nation.

God does not answer us because we hold Him accountable to a list of promises, but because of His own character and predisposition to love us. When a baby is hungry or in pain it does not have to recite a list of parental responsibilities; the parent does what is best for the child based on their love for them. In fact, the baby may not even know what is best or what it really needs, just as we don't always know what is best for us. But God sees and knows not only what we need but all the implications of the answers He gives.

The greatest asset we possess in times of trouble is the promise of God Himself. As Jehoshaphat prepared to offer his petition to God, he began by declaring what he knows about Him. What he declares to God becomes the basis upon which God will answer the petitions Jehoshaphat will offer. Jehoshaphat begins by declaring, *"You are the God of our fathers,"* which is another way of saying that God is faithful.

God is Faithful

The greatest encouragement we can find that God will address our present problems is to remind ourselves that He has intervened in the past. Jehoshaphat began his assault on God's throne by recognizing God's faithfulness to His people. The God of their fathers was with them in every kind of circumstance, and in every kind of trouble He was faithful. Jehoshaphat was declaring that God was with them before and would be now when the enemy was at the gate.

When God was about to deliver the nation of Israel from slavery He revealed Himself as the "God of his fathers." God said, "I am the God of your father—the God of Abraham, the God of Isaac, and the God of Jacob." (Exodus 3:5) When God refers to Himself as "the God of our fathers," He is manifesting Himself as the faithful Deliverer of His covenant people. He is saying, "I've done this before, and I am here to do it again." In the case of Israel, God was aware of their four hundred years spent in bondage, just as He knows that your business is in trouble or the challenges that face you as a parent. God is here to tell you that He knows what is going on and that He is already moving in the situation. He is the God of our fathers—a faithful covenant keeping God who never stops moving though we may not always be aware of His stirrings.

When confronted by a new enemy, Jehoshaphat could look back and see God's hand all over the history of His people. It was the God of their fathers who brought them out of the bitterness of slavery in Egypt. It was the God of their fathers who parted the Red Sea when Pharaoh's army was hot on their heels. It was the God of their fathers who brought forth water out of a rock and littered the desert with the bread of Heaven to sustain them in their wanderings. At every turn it was the God of their fathers who delivered them, though they may not have always understood or appreciated His methods or purpose.

Because God is the God of our fathers, the God who has been faithfully with us in trouble, we can look back at His faithful involvement and recognize His presence with us in our current situation. If God was with me when I lost my job He will be with me if I lose a car. If God, who is faithful, was with me when I was young and confused, He will be with me when I am old and feeble. God says, *"He shall call upon Me, and I will answer him; I will be with him in trouble; I will deliver him and honor him."* (Psalm 91:15)

God is faithful and reigns over every circumstance and situation. To the faithfulness

51

of God Jehoshaphat adds that God is the "God of Heaven"—God is Powerful

God is Powerful

After Jehoshaphat established the faithfulness of God over all kinds of circumstances, he asks God, "Art not thou God in Heaven?" Jehoshaphat acknowledges that God is above all other powers and influences, therefore, we must seek God before anyone or anything else. Jehoshaphat knew that the Torah said God was *"God in heaven above and on the earth beneath; there is no other."* (Deuteronomy 4:39) He was recognizing that ultimately everything and everybody is subject to God. It is God who holds the ultimate power over any possible circumstances, and nothing can happen that God does not allow. We must believe that ultimately God will prevail.

No situation is beyond God's power. We might have one son in prison and one son in ministry—one daughter a missionary and another who has two children before she's 22 without a husband. We may be celebrating with one and crying over the other, but God is the "God in Heaven." His purpose is not going to be thwarted by any other power in Heaven or earth. He will ultimately prevail.

52

He can bring those children back from the wake of disaster. He is not bound by our expectations or limitations.

God tells us to come boldly to His throne of grace. His throne is the seat of His power and authority over Heaven and Earth. We don't have to spend time going from counselor to psychologist to get an answer or find a healing. God is the source of all healing and we seek Him first. It is not that we cannot seek help from worldly sources, but to seek any other solution first is idolatry. Though God may use various means to deal with our problem, we must seek Him first. God may indeed use a doctor to heal our cancer, but we must ask Him for the name of the doctor. God is the God above all gods; the gods of humanism, the gods of philosophy, the gods of medicine, or any others we would care to name. We go to His throne—His seat of power and authority to find grace to swim through deep waters. God is the God above all—God is powerful.

Power means nothing unless the one who yields that power is predisposed to use it. God is not only willing, He is able to use it anywhere and any time He desires. God is the King—God is sovereign.

God is Sovereign

There are many levels and dimensions of authority that surround us, but all are subject to God. God is the Sovereign—the King over all of them. There are many thrones and dominions in the world, but all must take their places at the feet on God's throne. Jehoshaphat says, "Don't you rule over the kingdoms of the nations?" Certainly, you are comforted as I am by the writings of Daniel as he too makes that point clear by saying, "*the most high ruleth in the kingdom of men and giveth it to whomsoever He will.*" (Daniel 4:17)

We may look at these the powerful authorities that seem to be opposed to us or even to God's purpose. We look at the Iron Curtain that divided Europe after World War 2 and see that it seemed to be insurmountable to us. The Soviets had vast armies and nuclear weapons aimed at us. We were locked in a cold war with this powerful enemy for which we spent billions of dollars and many lives. We built fallout shelters and raised the stockpile of our own arsenals. In the end, however, that war was decided not by man's weapons but by God's will. It was prayer and the power of God that broke the back of the Soviet block. Thousands of unarmed people in public places raised the name of Him the Lord Jesus Christ and the walls fell. There were no siege machines or atomic threats; God just said, "That's enough", and the Iron Curtain fell.

It is God who sets up the kingdoms of the earth whether we perceive them as good or evil. God caused nations to rise and fall—He causes laws to be stricken. The Bible tells us that all authority is subject to God. Paul instructs the church concerning authority saying, "...there is no authority except from God, and the authorities that exist are appointed by God. (Romans 13:1) The tragedy of slavery and racial segregation ran their course in this nation, but God our Sovereign said, "That's enough." Apartheid was the a blight on South Africa for many years and could have ended much sooner, but it ended when God said it was time as suddenly as the Soviet block came apart. All of these are in the mighty hand of God. Has prejudice and injustice ended? Certainly not. But God is Sovereign over all kinds of injustices and they will all cease to the glory of God.

There is no demon that God does not know by name. There is no leader in power over any nation that can sit against the will of God. No terrorist, no name, no government can exert themselves against the faithfulness, power and sovereignty of God. In His hand is power and might that none can withstand. God is faithful, God is powerful, God is sovereign and will use His omnipotence on our behalf according to His purpose.

It is important for us to know that God reigns over all the nations as Sovereign, but we may ask, "What about me—what about my personal struggles? To this issue Jehoshaphat adds that God is "our God." God is not only sovereign over the nation in a corporate sense. God is Personal.

God Is Personal

Jehoshaphat states that God is "our God." God has this astounding way of being powerful to the extent that He can create the world or destroy nations while at the same time being incredibly tender with us on an individual basis. He makes His covenant with each of us personally just as He did at first with Abraham. He says to us as He did to Abraham, *"I will establish My covenant between Me and you..."* (Genesis 17:7) God's global strategy never supplants his love for each of us. God does not pave a road to world domination with the bones of lesser important people. He conquers it one heart at a time.

It must have driven both the Pharisees and disciples crazy when Jesus stopped to pick

up one child and bless them. (Mark 10:13-16)
There was no agenda—no appointment that
was more important than one child to Jesus.
He could have waved His arm and given them
a group blessing, but He chose to pick them up
and bless them one by one, just as He does with
us. God knows us all one at a time—calls us
one at a time—saves us one at a time—loves us
one at a time as individual children. While we
may have more than one child, no one is more
important to us than the other. We love all of
our children as individuals for themselves
alone.

God has chosen sides in the struggles we
face and the side He is on is ours. He is for us!
The neighborhood bully is not going to take
our lunch money for long. We are not alone in
whatever struggle we find ourselves. God is
our God and He relates to me as His friend—
someone who is in on His plan. God is not
only with us individually, He has chosen to
love us and bless us individually because He is
"our God."

Our God is faithful, powerful, sovereign,
and personal, but perhaps the most encouraging
thing that we can hold on to in the midst of
trouble is that our God is Present.

God Is Present

The greatest fear that any of us have as we face a challenge is that we are in trouble alone—that God is not there. Its one thing to find our finances in trouble, but quite another matter to believe that God has left us alone with an overdrawn bank account. Above all other attributes and characteristics of God, He wants us to know that He is a God who is present. When we are in that place of difficulty God declares that we can rely on His presence. He says, *"He shall call upon Me, and I will answer him; I will be with him in trouble; I will deliver him and honor him."* (Psalm 91:15)

Our fear that God is not with us is the direct result of man's fall into sin and his separation from God. But God, who could not stand to leave us alone any more than we could leave our own children alone in the Mall, left Heaven and joined us in the Person of Jesus Christ. The God in Heaven who was above all became Immanuel: *"God with us."* When things get hot we may not be able to find God with both hands. God may indeed seem far away, but He is a *"very present help in time of trouble."* (Psalm 46:1) The side column notes in the New American Standard translation suggest that a more accurate translation would be that God is *"abundantly available for help in tight places.*" What a powerful thought that the tighter things get the more available God is. The fear that we are alone without God is dealt a death-blow in the presence of Jesus Christ.

What we really want to know is that there is someone who hears us and understands us—someone who we can break down in front of and pour out our hearts. It maybe ok with us that God does not answer the way we would like as long as we know that we have been heard by Him, and that God is already moving on our behalf. It reminds me of when our kids were sick and we had to take them to the doctor. Maybe they would have to get a shot or be in pain until the sickness passed, but we were with them the whole time. Our *God is Present.*

What do these things have to do with the fairness of God?

When I encounter an enemy attack and I am tempted to believe that somehow God does not care, I become aware that my spirit is pulling me somewhere that my soul is tired of pressing through darkness for. My soul says that I'm tired and then I remember God told me to stop struggling in my own strength and know Him. (Psalm 46:10) I don't need to know that God created the world; I just need to experience Him. I don't need a lecture on Christology. I just need Him. What I long for more than any answer is the promise of God Himself in the midst of my trial. When I have the promise of all God is, I can expand my trust beyond my present experience and just be His. My worship becomes a litany of who God is rather than what He has done. As I experience Him in those tight places my knowledge of Him grows and I no longer need to hold onto promises of God because I have the promise of God Himself. Now I can wade into the deep end of the pool and swim in His presence. I can sense His presence and swim when the water is over my head and I cannot touch the bottom of the pool.

Now that I have the promise of God I cease trying to measure the fairness of God by my own human standards and understanding. God has become my faithful source, the power perfected in my weakness, my Sovereign Lord, my personal savior, and my present help. Now, with the promise of God Himself, I can leave my petitions at His feet and be sure of His love and compassion toward me. He has become my God, and I will ever praise Him!

CHAPTER SIX

The Next Move of God

*10 And now, behold, the children of
Ammon and Moab and mount Seir,
whom thou wouldest not let Israel
invade, when they came out of the land
of Egypt, but they turned from them, and
destroyed them not; 11 Behold, I say,
how they reward us, to come to cast us
out of thy possession, which thou hast
given us to inherit. 12 O our God, wilt
thou not judge them? for we have no
might against this great company that
cometh against us; neither know we
what to do: but our eyes are upon thee.*
(2 Chronicles 20:10-12)

"Behold." It's a word that ushers in new
reality—new seasons in God. *"Behold, a virgin
shall be with child..."* (Isaiah 7:14) or *"Behold, the days are coming, says the LORD,
when I will make a new covenant with the
house of Israel and with the house of Judah..."*
(Jeremiah 31:31). When we see the word
behold, we are entering new realms of relationship and experience in God. Our *beholds* are
places where God is being revealed.

Jehoshaphat was facing one of those *beholds* when he prayed, *"And now, behold, the chil- dren of Ammon and Moab and mount Seir..."*

Our *beholds* serve as introductions to life in a realm where we can love our enemies and where we can pray for those who misuse our kindness for their own purposes—a place where we can hold the fire of our own will and wait for God's. Our places of crisis or attack are places where we fall into the *purpose* of God, the *possession* of God, the *judgment* of God, the *wisdom* of God, and the *power* of God. They are the *"next moves of God"* in our lives. In these places of introduction God is doing something powerful—something that will bring Him glory and reveal new vistas of His love and grace.

When I am confronted and confounded by what seems to be unfair or uncomfortable for me, I have learned that I have come to the place of exchange. I am exchanging something of mine for something more powerful from God. The first thing I exchange is my purpose for God's. I realize it is *God's purpose, not mine* being served by this challenge in my life.

It's God's Purpose, Not Mine

Jehoshaphat reminded God that He did

not allow Israel to invade the territory of Ammon or Moab when they came out of captivity. God had His own purpose for Ammon and Moab that did not concern Israel. His purpose is not always obvious to us. In fact, it does not always appear that there is any kind of purpose being served in our times of stress. We have a tendency to be nearsighted, considering only our own lives and comfort. But very often God's purpose is being unfolded in the midst of our inconvenience.

When Moses led Israel to the brink of the Holy Land it seemed most expedient to cross through the territory of the Moabites and Ammonites. Moses perceived that it would suit God's purpose to get on with the business of inheriting the land of promise. But God had a different opinion and another agenda. The Lord said, *"Do not harass Moab, nor provoke them to war, for I will not give you any of their land as a possession, because I have given Ar to the sons of Lot as a possession."* (Deuteronomy 2:9) Instead of moving directly into the holy land God led his people to Kadesh: a place of separation.

The apparent diversion from God's ultimate plan for Israel was in fact a way to separate God's people from their own carnal tendencies so they could move into God's purpose of devoted fellowship. They had to be separated from their acquired appetites for the food of their slavery to the provision of Heaven.

Israel spent the first days out of captivity whining about the menu of God's provision. They recalled the cucumbers, leeks, onions and garlic that were theirs in bondage. (Numbers 11:5) Isn't it peculiar that they would long for a salad that would give them bad breath and a bellyache? God was taking them to a place flowing with abundance of every kind and description and they were moaning about an all you can eat trip to the salad bar. Many times those things we want to hang onto are so much inferior to what God has in mind. Sometimes we are being separated from our own puny appetites while God has planned an elaborate banquet.

Kadesh was also the place where God was separating His people from the rebellion in their hearts. It was a place where obedience was learned at the price of human ambition. (Numbers 12:14,16) There was rebellion at every turn whether from Moses' own brother and sister, or from Korah and his fellow mutineers. It was at Kadesh that all disobedience and disbelief was going to be removed from God's people. Obedience is in fact keeping our eyes on God instead of ourselves—His purpose rather than ours. God could not bring a rebellious nation into His inheritance; they would never survive.

He will also separate us from our own ambition and abilities to a place where we must rely on Him. We can get distracted from God's best for us. If we are to serve God's purpose, we must be separated from our own appetites and opinions and ability. God says, *"yea, I have spoken it, I will also bring it to pass; I have purposed it, I will also do it."* (Isaiah 46:11 KJV)

It's God's Possession, Not Mine

This is the place where we realize; I have exchanged my purpose for God's purpose. But God has exchanged all my old stuff for better and more eternal stuff. I have not lost anything I needed; neither can I ever lose it.

He said, *"they've come to throw us out of your possession."* It was never mine—it was yours and you trusted me with it. So I set myself to give a report that I'm losing your stuff because I gave you all of mine when I surrendered my life and was born again. When I came to you I came with my sinful self and you exchanged it for your righteousness. Maybe I came with drugs, or lying or gambling or lust, but you gave me purity in exchange. I didn't have anything worth saving and I gave you everything at the altar and walked away empty but filled. So, everything I have now, you gave me.

The enemy can touch nothing we have of any significance. Circumstances and stress may try to drive us out of our freedom, or our joy, or our worship, but those things are God's and cannot be tampered with. I cannot lose any of that if Walls Street falters and fails. And since all that we have is God's He will not allow us to try to preserve it by our own means. He will not allow me to cheat on my income taxes. He will not encourage me to steal or play the lottery. Whatever I have is from God and no one can take it out of His hand! So if He decides to take it away, then I don't need it anymore.

All that I have is from God—for God. *"His divine power has given to us all things that pertain to life and godliness, through the knowledge of Him who called us by glory and virtue..."* (2 Peter 1:3) If I don't have it, then I don't need it. The enemy cannot take anything out of God's hands He does not allow him to take. *It's God's possession, not mine.*

It's God's Judgment, Not Mine

Perhaps the first thing you and I do when confronted with some new tragedy is to make a decision whether it is a good thing or a bad thing. The problem is that we are trying to decide something that we cannot possible see from our limited perspective. In fact, we are trying to judge God, not the circumstance. When something good happens we say, *"God is good!"* When something happens that we perceive as bad we say, *"Where is God?"* In effect, we are judging God based upon circumstantial evidence. If we are comfortable God is good; if not, He is absent. None of us would be so bold to say that God is bad.

Jehoshaphat asked God, *"O our God, wilt thou not judge them?"* This seems to be a contradiction in one sentence. If God is God, He has already judged the circumstances and found them tenable, thus they have come our way. God, our God, has some purpose to serve in the midst of what seems unfair to us.

To judge anything we have to be able to see it completely. We are not in position to see all that God is doing, so we are not in a position to judge Him. We spoke in chapter one about our loss of a building that was to accommodate our growing congregation. But in reality, that building could not contain all that

God was planning to do. It is only now, after we have seen God's plan unfold that I realize how misplaced my disappointment was in losing that facility. God was doing something far greater than we first understood, and we had to be separated from our own ability and ambition to enter fully into what God had in mind. I was not in a position to judge God because I could not see all that He had in mind for us. Praise God that He will not allow us to settle for less than His best.

It's God's Power and Wisdom, Not Mine

When misery is in our face and we don't seem to have the ability to understanding or see our way through, God may have us just where He wants us. Until we reach the end of our power we cannot avail ourselves of God's power. Until we stop trying to figure everything out, we cannot hear from God. There is seldom room in our hearts and heads for more than one voice at a time.

We cannot hope to be aware of all the plans of the enemy that we will face. Jehoshaphat goes on to confess, "for we have no might against this great company that cometh against us, neither do we know what to do." We can't see every terrorist and every threat poised against us. Who would have thought on September 11, 2001 that some deranged maniacs would look at an airplane and see a weapon? We stood helplessly by watching thousands perish on national television. But even in that horrible scene God's power and wisdom was at work.

There was a film available after the tragedy that demonstrated God's intervening power and wisdom. A woman had more or less fallen into the doorway of a small store front that was occupied by a few other frightened people. What she did not know—what she did not see was the suffocating pestilence of a debris cloud that was close behind her. Those in the building who had pulled her into the safety of that storefront saw it coming they were the power and wisdom of God in that woman's life. As they all watched the smothering cloud pass by the woman suddenly she realized her salvation from certain death and cried out, *"Oh my God—Oh my God! Thank you—thank you!"* It was the wisdom and power of God at work in the worst of circumstances. Why God did not intervene a few hours earlier we cannot say, but God never stopped moving on our behalf.

The Apostle Paul has the eternal understanding on God's power and wisdom in our seasons of trial. He speaks to the Lord out of ecstatic praise at the various thorns stuck in his flesh. He heard God say to him, *"My grace is*

69

*sufficient for you, for My strength is made
perfect in weakness." Therefore most gladly I
will rather boast in my infirmities, that the
power of Christ may rest upon me. Therefore I
take pleasure in infirmities, in reproaches, in
needs, in persecutions, in distresses, for
Christ's sake. For when I am weak, then I am
strong.* (2 Corinthians 12:9-10) What a radical
perspective; strength out of weakness. It is
precisely when our strength is depleted that
God's enabling grace begins. We can in fact
then boast in things like "persecutions" because
God's purpose is being served. The most ma-
ture and faith-filled position on the seasons of
apparent unfairness sees them as opportunities
for the glory of God.

As we look at our trials through the eyes
of God we are engaged in several exchanges.
It's God's purpose, not ours—God's possession, not ours—God's judgment, not ours—
God's power and wisdom, not ours. The only
way we can find ourselves on the winning end
of these divine exchanges is to do what
Jehoshaphat says as he concludes his petition.
We must keep our eyes on God and leave the
next move to Him.

It's God's Move, Not Mine

Our eyes are on Thee…God, I'm paying
attention—I'm looking to see your purpose
manifested. All that I have is in your hands.

Our *beholds* are the place of God's next move. I don't always know how to interpret what appear to be negative happenings in my life, but I know that God is moving in the midst of them. They are places of His purposeful moving, His taking possession—His righteous and informed judgment—and His prevailing power and wisdom.

Whatever is in your face right now is an opportunity to observe the moving of God. Keep your eyes on Him. What He does next will reveal His heart and draw you closer to Him. It is the next move of God in your life.

> *To You I lift up my eyes, O You who are enthroned in the heavens! Behold, as the eyes of servants look to the hand of their master, As the eyes of a maid to the hand of her mistress, So our eyes look to the LORD our God, Until He is gracious to us.* (Psalm 123:1-2)

CHAPTER SEVEN

Standing Still On Shaky Ground

14 Then the Spirit of the LORD came upon Jahaziel the son of Zechariah, the son of Benaiah, the son of Jeiel, the son of Mattaniah, a Levite of the sons of Asaph, in the midst of the assembly. 15 And he said, "Listen, all you of Judah and you inhabitants of Jerusalem, and you, King Jehoshaphat! Thus says the LORD to you: 'Do not be afraid nor dismayed because of this great multitude, for the battle is not yours, but God's. 16 Tomorrow go down against them. They will surely come up by the Ascent of Ziz, and you will find them at the end of the brook before the Wilderness of Jeruel. 17 You will not need to fight in this battle. Position yourselves, stand still and see the salvation of the LORD, who is with you, O Judah and Jerusalem!' Do not fear or be dismayed; tomorrow go out against them, for the LORD is with you."
(2 Chronicles 20:14-17)

It is inevitable that you and I are going to experience times when all that we understood about God seems to become unsettled. Events are going to unfold before us that do not seem to square with what seems to be fair and right given the lives we have lived before God. The ground upon which we have stood becomes shaky at best.

So far, we have been doing all the talking and fretting, but now it's God's turn to talk and bring some kind of order to the chaos that surrounds us. Jehoshaphat and the people of Judah had gotten themselves into the proper position physically, mentally, and spiritually, and were now ready to hear from God. As God opened the mouth of the prophet, He spoke three imperatives for us to follow when confronted by circumstances that seem to be unfair. We need to *Listen up, Go down, and Stand still.* All of these enable us to keep our balance and stand still on shaky ground.

Listen up!

When God begins to speak into our new place in Him, He will probably speak to us in terms that are also new to us. In these times

God reveals something new about Himself so we need to listen carefully. This is a place where total and instant obedience to His voice will make the difference between glory and defeat. The Greek word for obedience is *hupakouo*, or literally to *listen up*. Listening is the first imperative in the midst of the unfamiliar.

This reminds me of the wedding feast at Cana at which Jesus performed the first miracle recorded in the Gospels. (John 2) They had run out of wine, a tight spot for the host of a wedding feast. In those days the whole village was invited to celebrate the wedding of two people getting married. It seems like more folks showed up than they expected and the supply of wine was insufficient. Though not exactly an enemy attack, it was a circumstance that could have been more than embarrassing for the host family. Mary, the mother of Jesus became aware of the shortfall and went directly to the only one who could help—Jesus.

The critical element in turning disaster into celebration was listening to Jesus. Mary told those in charge to *"Do whatever Jesus told them to do."* (John 2:5) Who had ever turned water into wine or anything else for that matter? They were told to fill large stone water pots used for ceremonial purification with water. To be sure, Jesus' instructions to them would have sounded crazy, but they listened and wine displaced what was water only moments earlier.

When we are in this new place we must learn to listen and then do whatever the Lord says, whether it makes sense or not, knowing that God is already at work right in the middle of that place. As we said in an earlier chapter, we are in a new place we built for God. Before anything else can happen we have to *listen*—to pay attention to what God is showing us.

Go Down!

When we read that God told Jehoshaphat and Judah to "go down" against the enemy, we would be tempted to think that God was trying out some kind of new shock therapy to overcome fear. God was telling a besieged nation to go down against an enemy many times their size and strength. God is saying, *"Forget that you are outnumbered...never mind that three invading armies are coming against your rag tag little puny army. "Go down against them...Get aggressive...Attack!!*

This sounds brave and noble, but its hard for an army to march out against an enemy that outnumbers them 3 to 1 when their knees are knocking in fear. We have to do something about the fear before we can do anything about the enemy. God has a word for us when we are outnumbered. *"Don't be afraid...this is My battle."*

When we find ourselves challenged or threatened by what we do not understand, we want to know whether or not anyone, particularly God, is paying attention—does anyone really care about what is happening to us—does anybody *see* the stuff we are in up to our necks? After all we have discussed, after we have set ourselves and prepared our minds to deal with the crisis at hand, we still want to know, *"Is anybody up there seeing what is going on down here?"*

God spoke to them in clear and unambiguous terms through one of His temple servants, Jahaziel, whose name could be interpreted as *"God sees."* God was not an absent landlord or a careless parent to them or us. God *sees* where we are and now begins to speak order into what feels like total chaos and unfairness. God *sees* the enemy that confronts us. He is not aghast and intimidated by what seems to be overwhelming odds. God sees and He is not afraid. Why should we be?

We need not be afraid because we are not alone. God says, "Don't be afraid or shake in fear, because I Myself am in the middle of the situation. I am here." How many times throughout the Bible does God comfort us when we are faced with fear by telling us that He is right here with us?

- To Abraham, *"Do not be afraid, Abram. I am your shield,"* Genesis 15:1
- To Isaac, *I am the God of your father Abraham; do not fear, for I am with you."* Genesis 26:24
- To the nation of Israel, *"Only do not rebel against the LORD, nor fear the people of the land, for they are our bread; their protection has departed from them, and the LORD is with us."* Numbers 14:9
- From the prophet to the exiled nation, *"Fear not, for I am with you;"* Isaiah 43:5

God's remedy for our shaking knees is His own presence with us. What enemy can we not face with Emmanuel, God with us, at our side? He is like the big brother who appears around the corner when the bully is about to knock our brains out. He is there…He is here. He has the bully by the throat. Do not be afraid. *Go down* against the enemy. *Attack*!!

We also need not to be afraid because we are meeting the enemy on God's own turf. He told Judah that the enemy would come up *before the Wilderness of Jeruel.* Jeruel could be interpreted as a place *"founded by God."*

God has seen this day approaching from the beginning; He is not surprised. Nothing or no one can sneak up on God. Who knows that perhaps God's purpose for not allowing Israel to attack Moab or Ammon on the way to Holy Land was because He saw this day when they would provide a good object lesson in trusting God? Whatever you are confronting may be used of God to draw you even closer to Him— to give a greater revelation of His glory and grace. Whatever the struggle or unfairness you face, it is being faced on ground that has been chosen by God, in His back yard.

We can *"go down against the enemy,"* because it's His enemy, His presence, His battle, and His battleground. We need not be afraid. But what do we do when we get there into the fray? God tells us there is no need to fight, but to *"stand still."*

Stand Still!

"Standing still" doesn't sound like much of a strategy to win a war. It's the last thing we want to do. We want military maneuvers and the sounds of clanking armor and shouts of hardened troops. Our human nature tells us that we have to *do* something in order to win the fight—to gain control. Surely when things seem unfair we have to do something. We have to make it right. We have to gain control. We

79

just have to do something, to make some kind of move. But when God has taken the field the only thing for us to do is to *stand still* and watch Him crush the enemy.

When we have our backs to the wall and nothing makes sense it seems as though God has led us into a trap. Think of the nation of Israel, who came out of hundreds of years of bondage only to be pinned against the Red Sea with thousand of armed and angry Egyptians at their backs. They had followed the instructions of Moses, God's man. They have smeared the blood over the door posts of their homes and watched the angel of death Passover them. They have been called the chosen of God—His own people who He would take out of bondage and into their own land. They had waited so long for deliverance and now they must choose between drowning or slaughter at the hands of their former masters. *How can this be fair?*

Once again, God speaks through His servant Moses to tell Israel. Listen to this familiar strategy.

> *13 And Moses said to the people, "Do not be afraid. Stand still, and see the salvation of the LORD, which He will accomplish for you today. For the Egyptians whom you see today, you shall see again*

no more forever. 14 The LORD will fight
for you, and you shall hold your peace."
(Exodus 14:13-14)

In effect, God had lured the enemy into a trap. Bent by their own evil hearts and intentions, the Egyptians followed Israel to the brink of what seemed an impossible position. The nation was pinned against the Sea and it seemed there was no way out. Now it was God's turn to act. Once again, God did something He had never done before, and divided the waters to allow the safe escape of the Israelites and the certain destruction of the Egyptians.

What else could the Israelites have done? What kind of program could they have devised to avoid the evil intended for them. I wonder what kind of anger was burning in them as the Egyptians got closer and closer. They were ready to go back to bondage and accused God of plotting their certain demise.

What goes through our heads each time we judge God unfair? We think to ourselves that God has brought us into his confidence only to squash us like bugs. We are ready to go back to the lesser life of answers in the flesh in order to avoid making sense of things. We just want a comfortable life and a nice home and for God to just make things work out and then leave us alone. But God is not ready to give up so easily. God is ready to part the Red Sea.

As we stand still and stop trying to make everything fair we become aware that God is already moving. That wind that parted the Red sea did not blow up as it did with Charlton Heston waving his staff. The wind blew all night and parted the Sea (Exodus 14:21) God was already moving on their behalf before they sighted the Egyptians at their backs. God is also moving on our behalf. God's schedule and strategy may not fit ours, but you can bet that He is about to overwhelm the Egyptians who are hot on your heels, and *"you will see them again no more forever!"*

When God was done talking and Jehoshaphat and the nation of Judah believed Him, they bowed their heads to the ground and worshipped Him.

> *18 And Jehoshaphat bowed his head with his face to the ground, and all Judah and the inhabitants of Jerusalem bowed before the LORD, worshiping the LORD. 19 Then the Levites of the children of the Kohathites and of the children of the Korahites stood up to praise the LORD God of Israel with voices loud and high.* (2 Chronicles 20:18-19)

What other kind of response could we have but to praise God? It must have felt like a man who got the results of a CT Scan only to learn that his doctor's diagnosis of certain cancer and death was wrong. It must have felt like getting a letter from the IRS that said, "We made a mistake on your taxes and you have more money coming back." (That would really be a miracle.) God is already moving—the east wind is already blowing on the sea of circumstances in front of you. God is not unfair—He is just unfinished!

Whatever the Lord is doing in your life is an ongoing process. There are going to be times when things don't add up in your favor, but God is still moving. When He is finished, He will get the glory for whatever happens if we will but learn to *Listen up, Go Down,* and *Stand Still* to see His salvation. He will calm the tremors and we will be *standing still on shaky ground.*

CHAPTER EIGHT

Amen!

20 So they rose early in the morning and went out into the Wilderness of Tekoa; and as they went out, Jehoshaphat stood and said, "Hear me, O Judah and you inhabitants of Jerusalem: Believe in the LORD your God, and you shall be established; believe His prophets, and you shall prosper."   21 And when he had consulted with the people, he appointed those who should sing to the LORD, and who should praise the beauty of holiness, as they went out before the army and were saying: "Praise the LORD, For His mercy endures forever." (2 Chronicles 20:20-21)

The enemy that wages war against our peace is mostly our own opinion of the circumstance we are in. A godly spouse is diagnosed with cancer and we leap to the conclusion that we have missed God or that He missed us. Or maybe our kids get thrown out of school for using drugs and immediately all those teachings and seminars on raising Christian children come to mind. We followed all the points—we spent quality time with the family and there was still a major train wreck. Or maybe we spend years establishing a new church only to have some loose prophetic lips begin to flap. We loved, we served, we obeyed, we wept, but the ship turned over and disappeared beneath the latest charismatic wave. *How can any of this be fair?*

We seldom understand what God is up to or how He is up to it. We want to see everything work out in a neat and orderly fashion that makes some kind of sense to us. We want reciprocity— we do well and God does good back at us. We are in search of a "fair" God rather than a sovereign and just God. We want things to balance out —we want to feel good about our lives. But what if God does not bring the deliverance we crave? What if we have done everything right and our business fails or the church doesn't grow? The only and the best option we have when things seem unfair is to agree with God and believe that He God knows what He is doing. We must say *AMEN* to God's character and intentions toward us.

Saying AMEN to God

Jehoshaphat's counsel to the people was to "*believe in the Lord*" and the word He has sent through the prophets. In the Hebrew text

Jehoshaphat was telling the people to say *AMEN* to God—to agree with God. To say AMEN to the Lord is to agree with God—to endorse His plan. When someone says something we agree with we say *AMEN!* To believe God is to allow the matter to rest in His hands without trying to fix it ourselves. The temptation to improve or add to God's plan is a basic human tendency that springs from our old nature—the way we used to be. But in the end, as with anything we do out of that old man, we will find ourselves lied to and separated from God.

Let's be honest and admit that it's hard to say *AMEN* to God when the bank is about to fore-close on us. It's against our wiring to say *AMEN* to God when the ministry God has called us to falls into disrepute through no fault of our own. It seems foolish to say *AMEN* to God when events seem to move so overwhelmingly against what just seems right to us—what makes sense. But we cannot convict God on such flimsy and cir-cumstantial evidence. We have not lived long enough. We have not seen God's heart revealed.

We must see the small sequences and events of our lives in terms of eternity. In the end, we will discover that God's purpose was ongoing and that His love and commitment for us remained untouched by our trouble. There is a good chance that we will not see the total picture this side of Heaven. But there will come a time before the throne of God in eternity that we will see it and say with the myriads of thousands of others; *AMEN! AMEN!* The Lord God the Almighty reigns.

Spiritual maturity comes as we grow past the notion that God will answer us or cause everything to work out to suit our comfort or notion of fairness. He may not, then again He may. Regardless, the matter before us is in His hands to. To say AMEN to God is to agree that God has a plan and that regardless of the outcome or level of comfort we will give glory to God.

Part of the *AMEN* that Jehoshaphat spoke to the people surrounded by the enemy was that they should praise the Lord for the "*beauty of his holiness.*" Praise was the response to God's word of comfort to Judah as we stated in the previous chapter. But the counsel to praise in this specific way became a weapon in the mouths of the oppressed because they said *AMEN* to the holiness of God.

AMEN to the Holiness of God

When I consider some of the places I have found myself in, in both my personal life and my ministry, I become a little more aware of how Moses must have felt when God sent him to bring Israel out of bondage. (Exodus 3) Moses must have said something like, *"Let's get this straight God. You are sending me to ask this king to let your people leave and you are then going to harden his heart so that he won't do it. How does this make any kind of sense? It seems like the deck is already stacked against Me."*

The difference for Moses, as it is for us in this circumstance is in this fact we are in on this fact; that the ground Moses was standing on was *"holy ground."* (Exodus 3:5) It was a place that belonged to God, so whatever happened was on God's tab. This is why Judah praised the *"beauty of God's holiness."* In this praise they were declaring the battleground as holy to the Lord. The battle, along with the glory, belonged to God.

When we say that something is holy we are saying that it belongs to God; that it is set apart for Him alone; it either belongs to Him or it doesn't. When we are praising the *"beauty of His holiness"* we are praising the reality that the circumstance or the trouble or the perceived unfairness belongs to God, and whatever belongs to God will ultimately bring Him glory and praise.

The proof of God's delivering hand in theexodus from Egypt was that the nation would worship Him at the mountain of God. (Exodus 3:12) Belief led to worship, which in turn led to deliverance as it also does as we consign our seasons of perceived unfairness to God's holiness.

> *Give unto the LORD, O you mighty ones,*
> *Give unto the LORD glory and strength.*
> *Give unto the LORD the glory due to His*
> *name; Worship the LORD in the beauty of*
> *holiness.*(Psalm 29:1-2)

AMEN to the Presence of God

The people of Judah and Jerusalem were very specific in the praise of God. They used the phrase, *"The Lord is good and His mercy endures forever."* These are the words sung when God is taking up residence in a new dwelling. These were the words sung when the ark of God's presence moved into David's back yard on Mount Zion. (1 Chronicles 16:34) They were the words sung when the temple built by Solomon was dedicated. (2 Chronicles 5:13) When these words were spoken in unity by the priests they ushered in the manifest glory of God. They are the words of the presence and reign of a high and lofty, but also a nearby God. They do not call down the presence of God they acknowledge Him.

Whatever the circumstance we find ourselves in is already filled with the presence of God, but we must acknowledge Him to gain His divine perspective. The fact is, it means that we must readjust our focus. Most of the fear we experience in our circumstance stems from our lack of recognizing the presence of God. We do not see Him because we are looking for Him with human eyes. We are watching for Him to destroy the enemy in front of us while He is in fact laying an ambush for them in ways and places that we cannot see because we are looking elsewhere. We can't see when we don't look.

God will be revealed through the circumstance we are in. Paul says that we cannot compare the present circumstance with the ultimate glory of God. He says, *"I consider that the sufferings of this present time are not worthy to be compared with the glory which shall be revealed in us."* (Romans 8:18) The meaning is clear.

What seems to be a bad turn of events—an unfair response to our faithfulness is going to look puny next to the eternal benefit of what is revealed *in* us.

All of those outward crises are developing something eternal on the inside as we say AMEN to God and trust His sovereignty and utter goodness. The business failure we suffer may open the way to a greater ministry. The fire in the church facility may force you to move toward a greater facility to accommodate all that God is going to increase through your ministry. Then again, He may do none of these things, but in the end all of these things will lead to the reality that God is greater than our plans and our pains.

AMEN to the Grace of God

The focal point of their praise was the Hebrew word *Checed*, translated as grace or mercy. Grace is the covenant love of God that says He is for us regardless of how things look. Grace is the enabling power of God stemming from the covenant love of God that reveals the faithfulness and compassion of God. That is a mouthful. Allow me to slow down a bit.

When God makes a covenant with us He is the one who provides the means by which we fulfill all of its obligations. It's as though God tells us to go to the store to buy a loaf of bread, then hands us the cash and the keys to a car to where we want to go. It's His car—it's His mission. We need to pay attention to His instruction regardless of our own opinion.

It is the grace of God that holds us together and gets us out on the other side of the situations in which we find ourselves. James says *"He gives us more grace."* But that grace is only available to those who humble themselves and look to God. James adds, *"God resists the proud, but He gives grace to the humble."* (James 4:6) The entrée to God's power to see us through the circumstance is to lean on Him.

All that we ever will be for God is a product of His grace alone. We cannot even be saved or grow close to Him without His grace. But all of the grace is accessed by this simple fact that we must say AMEN to God. We are saved by grace through faith. We survive the trials we find ourselves in by grace through faith. We learn the heart of God as it is revealed to us by grace through faith. All of this only as we say AMEN to God.

When we have begun to agree with God—to say AMEN to our circumstances the Lord Himself takes up the battle. There will be no mixture of human dependence and the grace of God just as there will not be any mixture of glory to God and glory to us. It's all on God. AMEN!

CHAPTER NINE

Bushwhacked!

22 Now when they began to sing and to praise, the LORD set ambushes against the people of Ammon, Moab, and Mount Seir, who had come against Judah; and they were defeated. 23 For the people of Ammon and Moab stood up against the inhabitants of Mount Seir to utterly kill and destroy them. And when they had made an end of the inhabitants of Seir, they helped to destroy one another.
(2 Chronicles 20:22-23)

In the old Western we used to watch on Saturday mornings the times when the good guys would fall into a trap set by the bad guys. The bad guys would hide in the bushes and jump out with guns blazing against the good guys. The good guys were "bushwhacked." There was some kind of lethal surprise in store for the bushwhackee by the bushwhacker. Something they did not expect. God also had a surprise for those who attacked Judah as well. They were Bushwhacked!

95

When we have said AMEN to God, worshipped Him, given Him full reign, and consigned ourselves to His grace and glory, He takes the battle to the enemy. He will have the last laugh— He will say the last AMEN!

Those very circumstances that could have derailed us now begin to serve the purpose of God. The Psalm says, "God has spoken in His holiness: "Moab is My washpot; Over Edom I will cast My shoe..." (Psalm 108:7,9) In other words, Moab and Edom become the servants of God. Whatever the circumstance it will serve God. I don't always understand what is going on but it will serve God. I may not find results I want, but it will serve God.

The very things that could have driven us further from God now draw us closer to Him. We draw closer in dependence; closer in revelation; closer in intimate relationship with Him. It becomes as Joseph said, *"But as for you, you meant evil against me; but God meant it for good, in order to bring it about as it is this day, to save many people alive."* (Genesis 50:20-21)

It could not have been pleasant for Joseph to lie at the bottom of that dry well in Dothan at the hands of his brothers. He had done nothing to them but tell the truth as revealed by God. He did nothing to deserve such treatment and wounding. How could it have been fair? It was not pleasant in serving time in jail for denying the amorous advances of a middle-aged frustrated housewife. It just wasn't fair. But through it all, Joseph continued to say AMEN to God. The result was salvation to his people and glory to God without which you and I would not be writing or saying the words in this book.

As we trust the Lord the enemy of fear is bushwhacked! We can choose to either agree with the trouble or with God. The choice is up to us. If we want power we must open our mouths to say AMEN to God.

24 So when Judah came to a place overlooking the wilderness, they looked toward the multitude; and there were their dead bodies, fallen on the earth. No one had escaped. 25 When Jehoshaphat and his people came to take away their spoil, they found among them an abundance of valuables on the dead bodies, and precious jewelry, which they stripped off for themselves, more than they could carry away; and they were three days gathering the spoil because there was so much. 26 And on the fourth

97

*day they assembled in the Valley of
Berachah, for there they blessed the
LORD; therefore the name of that place
was called The Valley of Berachah until
this day. 27 Then they returned, every
man of Judah and Jerusalem, with
Jehoshaphat in front of them, to go back
to Jerusalem with joy, for the LORD had
made them rejoice over their enemies.
28 So they came to Jerusalem, with
stringed instruments and harps and
trumpets, to the house of the LORD. 29
And the fear of God was on all the
kingdoms of those countries when they
heard that the LORD had fought against
the enemies of Israel.* (2 Chronicles
20:24-29)

When the day is over and sun has set on
our trouble, God is going to get the glory and we
are going to get the spoil. The glory to be revealed is going to mute and dwarf the suffering
of our trouble.

As we consign ourselves to God's love in
the midst of trial we are removed from the do-
minion of circumstances in our lives. This is the
very definition of blessing. The blessing we find
as we say AMEN to God overwhelms the notion
of unfairness. We find ourselves beyond the

power of the enemy and no longer live under the circumstances. Nothing can harm us because it all belongs to God.

The net result of our *AMEN* to God is an awe of God that confronts those who see us going through the battle with nothing more than harps and trumpets. Our AMEN to God becomes an invitation to the world that will join us as we shout with one voice,

"Hallelujah! For the Lord our God, the Almighty, reigns" (Revelations 19:6)

---

[1] (Bible history Old Testament by Alfred Edersheim, The History of Judah and Israel. Chapter 6, page 79 William B. Eerdmans Publishing Company, Grand Rapids, Michigan)

DONALD A. WRIGHT

Bishop Donald Anthony Wright, was born and raised in Washington, DC. He began preaching in his early 20's and assumed his first pastorate shortly thereafter. Today, Bishop Wright is the proud Pastor of Jabbok International Fellowship, a rapidly growing congregation of more than 3,000 members. Jabbok is strategically located on the outskirts of the Nation's Capitol as a church with a burden to restore the power of prayer and worship and impact the world with a clear sound of the gospel of the Kingdom.

Bishop Wright serves as the Vice Presiding Bishop of the MECCA (Ministries of Excellence Challenging Christians to Advance) Fellowship, under the leadership of Bishop Andrew Turner. This fellowship consists of some 800 churches in over 20 nations.

As one who has a great compassion for the youth, In August, 2000, Bishop Wright single-handedly pioneered the first "Next Generation Youth Conference " which was held at the MCI Center in downtown, Washington, DC. This event brought together more than 15,000 young people from all over the United States to a day of nonstop prayer, praise and worship.

A central focus of Bishop Wright is that of inner healing which led to the publication of his best-seller book, "Tonight We Wrestle". He holds three doctorates in the areas of Theology, Ministry and Psychology.

Bishop Wright and his wife Sabrina have five children: Donita, Donald, Jr., Daron, Derrick and Antoine.